ISBN: 9798698645

Independently published by K

C000212885

Contents Page

Would you rather?

Would you rather sign for
Barcelona and never play in
the first team **OR** spend your
whole career in the
Championship but be a star?

Which would you rather
give up - supporting
your football team **OR**
your relationship?

Would you rather have England go out of every tournament on penalties forever **OR** have Germany win every World Cup for the rest of time?

Would you rather look like Cristiano Ronaldo and play like Jon Flanagan **OR** look like Jon Flanagan and play like Cristiano Ronaldo?

Would you rather lose the league and your rivals lose the Champions League final **OR** win the league but your rivals win the Champions League?

Would you rather score the winning goal in a World Cup final **OR** do the treble with your club?

4

Would you rather try to last one round in a boxing match with Adebayo Akinfenwa **OR** have to chew a handful of broken glass?

Would you rather let Wayne Rooney take your grandma on a date **OR** let John Terry have your wife's phone number?

Would you rather listen
to Michael Owen talk for
12 hours everyday **OR**
never watch football
again?

Would you rather be
twice the height of Peter
Crouch **OR** be half the
height Lionel Messi?

Would you rather stand in a wall for a Roberto Carlos free-kick **OR** go in for a 50/50 tackle with Roy Keane

Would you rather your team buy the title with foreign players **OR** stay mid-table but mostly bring through local, youth players

Would you rather not play a single minute and still win the Champions League **OR** miss a penalty in the final after being the best player?

Would you rather do a poo on the football pitch and no one saw **OR** not do a poo but everyone thought you did?

Who would you rather have in your midfield? Gerrard, Lampard **OR** Scholes?

Who would you rather have in your team for the next 10 years, Håland **OR** Mbappé?

Would you rather slip like Steven Gerrard in front of millions to cost your team the league **OR** wear a diaper for the rest of your life?

Would you rather have to share every meal you'll ever have with Ronaldo **OR** only eat Brussel sprouts for all time?

Would you rather have hair like Gervinho for the rest of your life **OR** lose a winning lottery ticket?

Would you rather wear the shirt of your most hated team everyday for five years **OR** have to sleep in a haunted house for 20 years?

Would you rather score the winning goal in the Europa League final **OR** make an appearance in the Champions League Final?

Whose haircut would you rather have for the rest of your life? Marouane Chamakh **OR** 2002 Ronaldo?

Would you rather
get a football lesson
from Zinedine Zidane
OR Ronaldinho?

Would you rather your
club signed Cristiano
Ronaldo **OR** Lionel Messi
in their prime?

Would you rather your club win the Champions League **OR** your country win the World Cup?

Would you rather score 15 goals in one season with no assists **OR** provide 25 assists and score no goals?

Would you rather score a hat-trick but lose the match **OR** win the game without scoring?

Would you rather score 15 goals in one season with no assists **OR** provide 25 assists and score no goals?

Would you rather never watch a football match on tv **OR** in a stadium ever again?

Would you rather play a football match barefoot **OR** with no shorts?

Would you rather play football in heavy rain **OR** strong winds?

Would you rather finish above your rivals but they do the double over you and knock you out **OR** a cup or visa versa?

Would you rather Jon Arne Riise strike a howitzer at you from 6 yards **OR** be slapped in the face by your partner?

Would you rather play a football match barefoot **OR** with no shorts?

Would you rather play in front of 100,000 in a stadium **OR** play in an empty stadium with 100 million people watching on tv?

Would you rather win the Premier League **OR** a Europa League, FA Cup, League Cup treble?

Would you rather your club win the Premier League and get relegated the next season **OR** get back to back top 4 finishes?

Would you rather break both your legs **OR** dislocate your knee?

Would you rather
play a full 90 in -5°C
OR 50°C?

Would you rather only play
for England **OR** only play in
the Championship?

Would you rather your favourite football league team drop out of the league and England win the world **OR** they stay put and England fail to qualify for the finals?

Would you rather only play for England **OR** only play in the Championship?

If a free kick going in meant you could spend one night with the man/woman of your dreams who would you rather have stood over it? David Beckham **OR** Juninho Pernambucano?

Would you rather Mario Balotelli host a firework party for you **OR** go shooting with Ashley Cole?

Would you rather be world class until 25 then be injured all the time **OR** be an unknown until 30 and then become world class?

Would you rather start a game 1-0 down with your best player **OR** 0-0 without?

Would you rather the opposition start a game with 10 men **OR** they start with every player on a yellow card?

Would you rather play for a team in a great city with a tiny stadium **OR** a terrible city with a world class stadium?

Would you rather your club have a laughable badge **OR** laughable kits?

Would you rather PSG **OR** Manchester City win their maiden champions league first?

In their primes; would you rather John Terry **OR** Rio Ferdinand in your side?

In their primes; would you rather Fernando Torres **OR** Luis Suárez in your side?

Rivalries

AC Milan
or
Inter?

Ajax or
Feynoord?

Arsenal

or

Spurs?

Athletic Bilbao

or

Real Sociedad?

Atlético Madrid
or
Real Madrid?

Benfica
or
Sporting Lisbon?

Borussia Dortmund
or
Schalke?

Cardiff City
or
Swansea City?

Kaizer Chiefs
or
Orlando Pirates?

Lyon
or
Saint-Etienne?

Marseille

or

PSG?

Newcastle

or

Sunderland?

Liverpool
or
Manchester United?

Olympiacos
or
Panathinaikos?

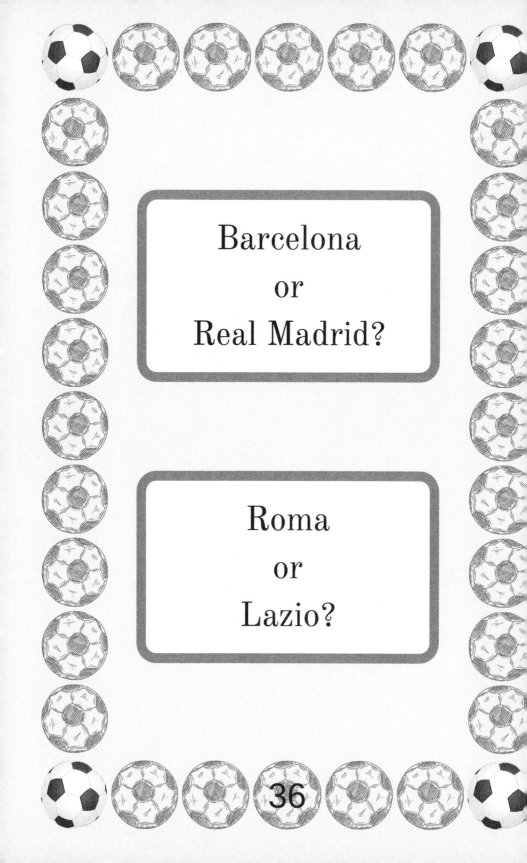

Barcelona
or
Real Madrid?

Roma
or
Lazio?

Bayern Munich
or
Borussia Dortmund

Galatasaray
or
Fenerbahçe?

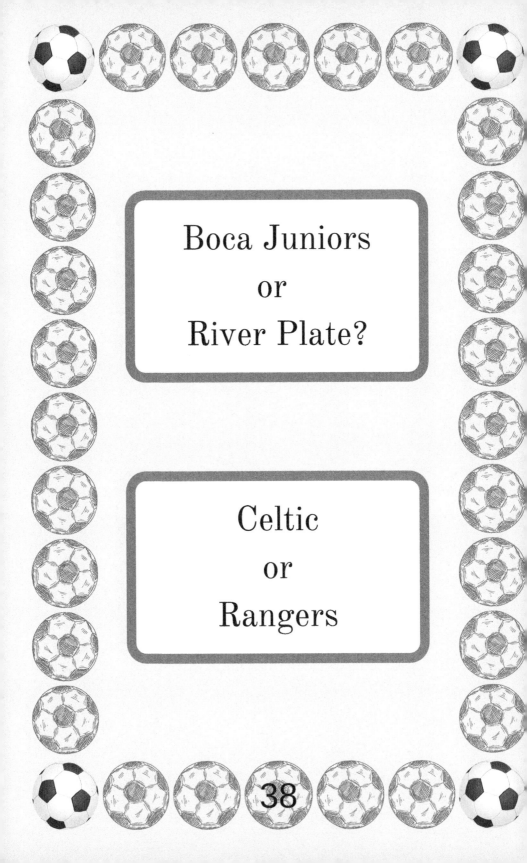

Boca Juniors
or
River Plate?

Celtic
or
Rangers

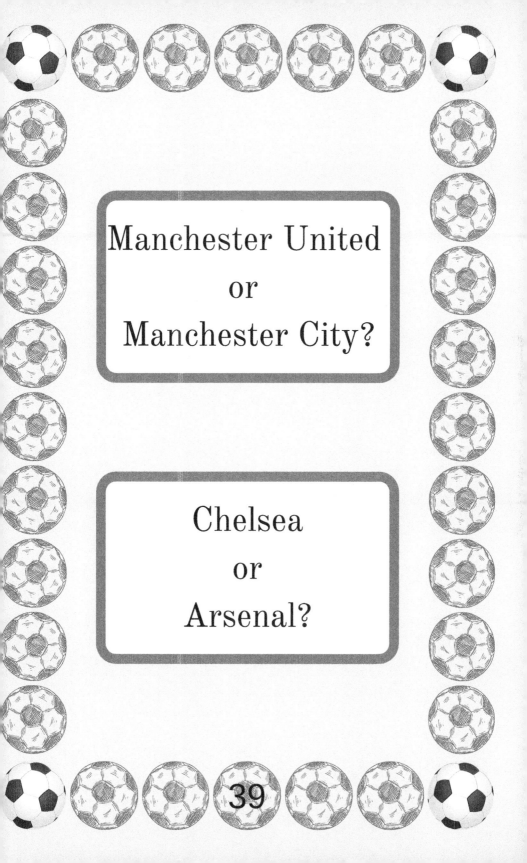

Manchester United
or
Manchester City?

Chelsea
or
Arsenal?

Sheffield United
or
Sheffield Wednesday?

Real Betis
or
Sevilla?

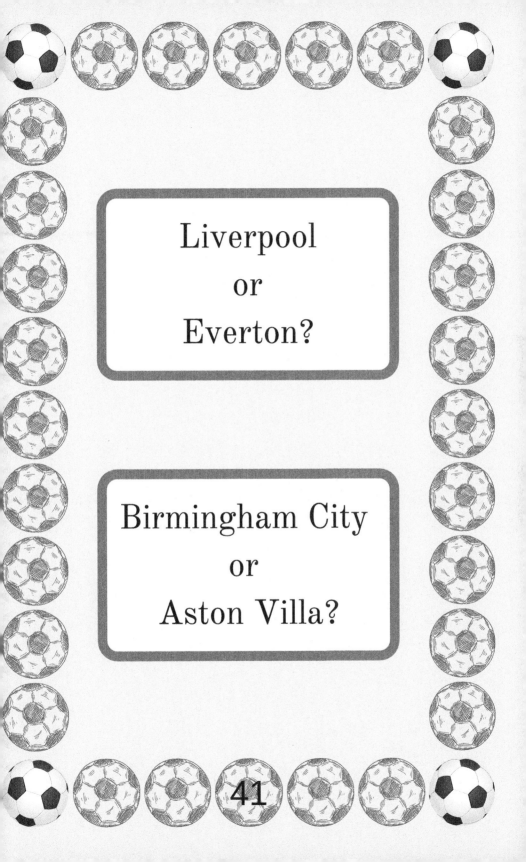

Liverpool
or
Everton?

Birmingham City
or
Aston Villa?

Portsmouth
or
Southampton?

Flamengo
or
Fluminese?

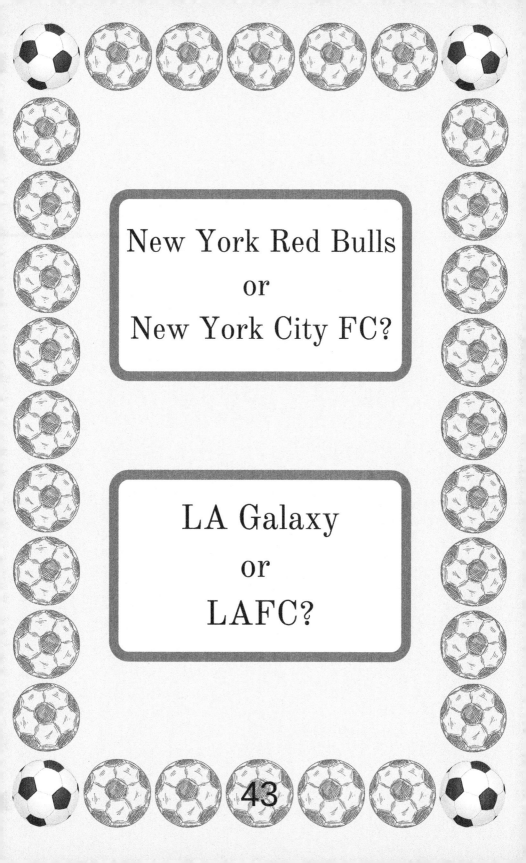

New York Red Bulls
or
New York City FC?

LA Galaxy
or
LAFC?

Pick Your All Time Greatest XI

Goalkeeper

Gianluigi
Buffon

Lev
Yashin

Peter
Schmeichel

Iker
Casillas

Right Back

Dani Alves

Cafu

Javier Zanetti

Carlos Alberto

Centre Back

Franz
Beckenbauer

Franco
Baresi

Sir Bobby
Moore

Alessandro
Nesta

Centre Back

Fabio Cannavaro

Sergio Ramos

Ronald Koeman

Carles Puyol

Left Back

Paolo
Maldini

Roberto
Carlos

Giacinto
Facchetti

Philip
Lahm

Midfielder

Zinedine Zidane

Xavi Hernández

Zico

Sir Bobby Charlton

Midfielder

Johan
Cruyff

Frank
Lampard

Andrés
Iniesta

Lothar
Matthäus

Midfielder

Steven Gerrard

Diego Maradona

Michel Platini

Frank Rijkaard

Right Winger

Lionel Messi

George Best

Ronaldinho

Garrincha

Left Winger

Cristiano
Ronaldo

Hristo
Stoichkov

Rivelino

Ryan
Giggs

Striker

Pelé

Ronaldo

Thierry
Henry

Gerd
Müller

Striker

Alan
Shearer

Eusébio

Wayne
Rooney

Ferenc
Puskás

Manager

Sir Alex Ferguson

Arsène Wenger

Carlo Ancelotti

Arrigo Sacchi

Manager

José
Mourinho

Pep
Guardiola

Bill
Shankly

Vicente
del Bosque

All Time Best XI

Goalkeeper
....

Right Back
....

Centre Back
....

Centre Back
....

Left Back
....

Midfielder
....

Midfielder
....

Midfielder
....

Right Winger
....

Striker
....

Left Winger
....

Manager
....

Current Best World XI

60

Goalkeeper

Manuel Neuer

Marc-André ter Stegen

Alisson Becker

Jan Oblak

Right Back

Trent Alexander-Arnold

Dani Carvajal

Joshua Kimmich

Kyle Walker

Centre Back

Virgil
van Dijk

Raphaël
Varane

Milan
Škriniar

David
Alaba

Centre Back

Aymeric Laporte

Leonardo Bonucci

Sergio Ramos

Kalidou Koulibaly

Left Back

Jordi
Alba

Andrew
Robertson

Alphonso
Davies

Alex
Sandro

Midfielder

N'Golo
Kante

Toni
Kroos

Kevin
De Bruyne

Frenkie
de Jong

Midfielder

Sergio
Busquets

Thiago
Alcântara

Luka
Modrić

Thomas
Müller

Right Winger

Serge
Gnabry

Lionel
Messi

Mohamed
Salah

Jadon
Sancho

Left Winger

Neymar

Cristiano Ronaldo

Eden Hazard

Sadio Mané

Striker

Robert
Lewandowski

Karim
Benzema

Sergio
Agüero

Harry
Kane

Striker

Pierre-Emerick
Aubameyang

Roberto
Firmino

Kylian
Mbappé

Romelu
Lukaku

Manager

Diego
Simeone

Pep
Guardiola

José
Mourinho

Jürgen
Klopp

Current Best XI

Goalkeeper
....

Right Back
....

Centre Back
....

Centre Back
....

Left Back
....

Midfielder
....

Midfielder
....

Midfielder
....

Right Winger
....

Striker
....

Left Winger
....

Manager
....

Debates

Did Wayne Rooney
fulfill his potential?

Was Barça 2011 the
greatest football side of
all time?

What is harder to win?
The Premier League or
the Champions
League?

Excluding Messi &
Ronaldo who is the
greatest footballer of
all time?

Who is the greatest
Premier League player
of all time?

Is VAR good for
football?

Did Marcus Rashford
deserve his MBE?

Who is England's
greatest footballer?

Should big clubs
support lower league
clubs financially?

Should the English
League Cup be
scrapped?

How could women's football be made more popular as a spectator sport?

Should draws be eliminated and penalties used to give a result for every game?

Should goals increase in size to allow more goals to be scored?

Should wage caps be introduced?

What are the disadvantages of playing football for a living?

Should there be any changes made to the extra time rule for knockout games?

Should there be playoffs for the final Champions League spot in the Premier League?

Should the World Cup be expanded to 64 teams?

Who is the greatest
goalkeeper of all time?

Who is the greatest
defender of all time?

Who is the greatest
midfielder of all time?

Who is the greatest
forward of all time?

And that's all folks! Thank you so much for purchasing and using this quiz book, I do hope you enjoyed the content and had some great football debates!

Don't forget to tell your friends and family about the book and If you like it I would really appreciate a review if you have the time!

Thanks again.